Spinning Straw Into Gold:

Straight Talk for
Troubled Times

Praise for Morris Berman and
Spinning Straw Into Gold

Over the decades, Morris Berman has provided readers with compelling books whose topics range from spiritual awareness to probing analysis of America's decline. In *Spinning Straw Into Gold* he explores his own life trajectory as he stepped away from society's traditional demands and measures of meaning, and found what was truly meaningful instead. The result is a powerful, timely, and mind-opening challenge for all of us to do the same.–

Nomi Prins, author of *It Takes a Pillage, Black Tuesday,* and other works.

~ ~

For years Morris Berman has been describing the downfall of America, an argument that shocked many by its apparent pessimism. But a sensitive reader will have discerned a very positive message at the bottom of his recent trilogy on the American decline: that we are the last survivors of a failed empire, and will witness the emergence of a better, more balanced relation to the world from the ruins of its destructive manias and obsessions. Berman writes in the tradition of Paul Goodman's *Growing Up Absurd*, Erich Fromm's *Escape from Freedom,* and the mother lode of all such individual wisdom in America, *The Adventures of Huckleberry Finn*. This is not your typical self-help manual, but a clear-headed, translucently reasoned account of how one individual broke free from a dysfunctional culture and now gives us a way to accomplish the same liberation for ourselves.–

Paul Christensen, author of *The Human Condition* and *Strangers in Paradise.*

Spinning Straw Into Gold:

Straight Talk for
Troubled Times

Morris Berman

Published by Echo Point Books & Media
Brattleboro, Vermont
www.EchoPointBooks.com

Spinning Straw into Gold
ISBN: 978-1-63561-053-6 (paperback)

Original Art by Samala Coffey

Cover design by Adrienne Núñez
Cover image: Good sunset over golden field with harvest,
© Mykola Mazuryk /shutterstock

Author photograph by John Trotter

There is no wealth but life.

–John Ruskin

It was not until I reached my mid-sixties that I began to have some insight into my own life, and (I like to think) life in general. Some say that we don't really know much of anything until we turn forty, but for me forty came and went without any great breakthroughs. Perhaps it just takes having the opportunity to slow down—an enormous luxury, in this day and age. I had just turned sixty-two when I crossed the border into Mexico, which I was determined to make my home; and it was a lucky decision, if luck had anything to do with it. But I did indeed slow down. I began to see more clearly who I was. I was able to just let my mind drift, go where it wanted to. Typically, the day began by making myself a strong cup of tea with milk and sugar, and then sitting on my couch and staring into space for an hour, or more if I felt like it. Or I would sit in my patio, watching green or vermillion-colored beetles crawling along the edges of my potted plants, or in my garden, observing the hummingbirds darting in and out among the flowers. If this was retirement, I couldn't get enough of it. Time stood still; things that used to bother me, suddenly didn't.

But "retirement" proved to be fairly busy, as it turned out, although (somehow) in a very relaxed way. Books just seemed to "fall out" of me. I wrote a novel, a volume of poetry, and a collection of essays—all of them ruminations on life, on what we were doing on this earth. There was no pressure; it was more a feeling of quiet immersion, and of contemplating things that I previously had very little time to reflect on.

One of the things I began to think about was the role of chance vs. fate in human life. They seemed twisted together, like strands of DNA. It hit me how driven our lives are by factors buried deep in our psyches, our genes, and our early childhoods; and how little we can do to change any of this. I looked back at epic struggles I had had in the past—a bad marriage (two people with nothing in common making each other miserable), moderate professional success (publications, the details of which I no longer remember; tenure, over which I sweated for months; invitations to lecture at conferences that were strange and/or boring), and seemingly endless personal conflicts over anything and everything (Dell sent my ink cartridges to the wrong address)—and much of it now seemed unnecessary in retrospect, a waste of time; stupid, even. I had the feeling that a lot of that wasted energy, those ultimately trivial struggles, could have been avoided if I had had the awareness at the time that it all really didn't matter, that I could have just "let the universe do its thing," and that what was supposed to work out in my favor, would.

The "stuckness" surrounding our behavior, the ruts we occupy and live out (or in), is of course easier to see in those around us, than in ourselves. The notion of "karma" itself seems overpowering, almost too amorphous to contemplate. Yet, you want to say to the other person—friend, lover, or whomever—"Don't you see? It's this pattern you've got to break. Move against your habitual mode of behavior, confront the anxiety, and you'll be better off." Sometimes these folks are twenty or thirty years younger than I, and I think: "Would *I* have taken such advice in my thirties or forties? *Did* I? Of course not. Like you, these folks are going to pursue the path they are on until they hit a wall, until whatever they've been doing doesn't work anymore." So for the most part I don't say anything, or offer advice that might fall on deaf ears. I just let nature (or karma) take its course.

Karma

Because karma affects one personally, it's something one learns, in one's sixties (perhaps a bit earlier for the more fortunate), to observe, see through, in one's own life and the lives of others. I kept wondering: "Can one change one's destiny as an act of will? Can one decide that they aren't happy with the path they are on, and deliberately leave it, take up a different path? Or that they don't like the cards they had been dealt, so to speak, and shuffle the deck and start over?" These questions swam around in my mind until they finally turned into stories, or novellas, that in turn wove together into a novel, of sorts, which enabled me to explore the options that human beings might have to live creatively different lives.

In the first story Jason Green, a rather timid librarian living in New York, is, like many of us, dissatisfied with his life—as I had been at various points in mine. He has this nagging feeling, and one that I suspect is hardly uncommon, that he's not living the life he was meant to live; that somewhere along the line he missed the boat. What he really wants is to start over: return to an earlier point in his life and try to do it differently this time around; do it "right." Lo and behold, he trips onto a meditation technique that enables him to do just that—time travel—and he finds himself back at age nineteen, but with the consciousness of a man in his fifties. And yet, the whole exercise eventually backfires. He is ultimately unable to manipulate events to his advantage, and has to reconcile himself with the fact that the life he has is as good as it's going to get.

Thoughts about a past love—one that didn't work out—led me to write the second story, which (despite the failure of the relationship) is a bit more optimistic. Fifteen years ago or so I had a girlfriend who was trapped in a way of being that compelled her to distance herself from everyone and everything around her, myself included, so that nothing was finally real for her. It was an anxiety reaction, a protective mechanism, and so effective that in a sense she wasn't really alive. Or it was a life that had played out, up to that point, inside of a glass box, so to speak. In the story—which consists of a long dream in which she breaks with her usual pattern of holding everything at arm's length—she awakes to realize that her very life is at stake, and sees that if she doesn't muster the courage to disrupt her normal conditioning, she will be trapped forever in a zombie-like existence. "Irene" didn't actually do this during the time that I knew her, but in the novella I wanted to give her the best chance possible: she faces her anxiety, and opens up to the possibility of becoming vulnerable to those around her. (She was forty then, close to sixty now; I'm hoping she made it.)

The third story was partly inspired by my life as a "retiree." I guess I may have been thinking about the directions my life could go in, now that I was relatively unencumbered. The central character is an American high school teacher (modeled on one of my own teachers, from way back when, and whom I always admired for his quiet humility) who accidentally writes a best-seller, the sales of which enable him to quit his job and move to a small town in England and reflect on his life up to that point. Somehow, he gets it into his head that he should try to perfect or "purify" his life by working his way through the Seven Deadly Sins: pride (ego), envy, anger, sloth, greed, gluttony, lust. At the point that the project starts to unravel in a comical kind of way, he meets another American expatriate, a woman with whom he falls in love, who shows him that the whole exercise is pointless: his life is "perfect" just as it is.

Thinking about it now, these tales call to mind that line from John Lennon, "Life is what's happening while you're making other plans." Who of us really knows what is best for us? What would it take to trust the unseen, the deeper forces that constitute a kind of guidance? How might we make ourselves available to those forces?

My entire life was changed by a shattering kind of "mystical-psychotic" experience I had shortly before my thirtieth birthday, triggered by a particular type of meditation practice I had recently embarked on. It was, quite frankly, an experience I would never wish to repeat. But it did manage to tear me out of habitual patterns that were turning my life into an embalmed existence, a kind of academic death-in-life. So what seemed like hell at the time ultimately proved to be salvation. We really don't know what's in our best interest. It certainly isn't our conscious or immediate impulses; of that I'm quite certain.

And now?, I sometimes ask myself; do you know *now?* Has age endowed you with the ability to see through your conscious desires to the deeper forces you need to pursue? Well, yes and no. I mean, it's better than it was thirty years ago; the time-gap of understanding is shorter; but there's still a gap.

Glimpses

I guess what I *can* say is that the years have provided me with a kind of "flashlight" for looking into what's going on with me, such that I experience two kinds of "glimpses" into the trajectory of my life, or destiny, from time to time. The first is an oblique awareness that I'm on the right track, though I can't say how I know this. It's as though there is a "vector" one can follow, which says: "Go this way." Yet, we sometimes hesitate; too often, we want to know that the outcome of moving in a particular direction will be successful, when in fact there is no way to know.

The "vector" is not about guarantees. What it does do is call on us to trust; and I am now convinced that this one single act, this leap of faith, is the most important act one can perform in one's life. Over and over, circumstances (or "the universe," if you prefer) will call on us to take this step, and it is here that we find the link between Chance and Fate: *you make your fate by taking the chance.* It's hard to see this, but it is deterministic and existential at the same time.

The second kind of glimpse is much more difficult to describe, because it is something like a vague body tremor, or wave of light, that passes through me, perhaps once or twice a month. It's very subtle, sort of peripheral, and I can never anticipate when it's going to "strike," or shimmer through my being. I'll be driving along, for example, and I'll check the rearview mirror, and suddenly it happens, like a luminous blink. Or I'll be sitting on my couch, writing in my notebook, and I'll look up for a moment and—there it is, a kind of flash. It lasts only two or three seconds, when it does occur, and the message is always the same: "Things are as they should be; the world is on your side." It's similar, in some ways, to the first type of glimpse, but a lot more impersonal. More like: "The world is doing what it has to do; don't worry too much about it."

The Vector

In any case, getting back to Chance and Fate, or the existential and the deterministic, four types of decisions have fallen into this category for me: what book I was going to write; what job I was going to take; which city I was going to live in; and which woman I was going to have a relationship with. These things chose me far more than I chose them. My role in all of these events was only to follow the "vector," that big arrow that says, "Right this way, amigo." To paraphrase the Rolling Stones, You don't always get what you want, but a lot of the time you get what you need. The point, again, is to trust what's happening, and thus, to endure it. Sadness, for example, has an important function in our lives; suppressing it with drugs or compulsive activity is not the best way to deal with it. Instead, we need to embrace it or connect with it, sit with it, breathe it in. Because on the other side of sadness there exists a "farther shore," one that binds that sadness to the next step in our lives, the new direction.

Nothing lasts forever except one thing, if you commit yourself to it: awareness. Through that, one can arrive at a deeper sense of the world, and a deeper appreciation of oneself. And if one cannot see the meaning of things right in the moment, while they are happening, it's also the case that the gap between event and understanding may get narrower as one gets older. Trust, patience, and endurance make this possible.

The Accident

I was sixty-seven years old when quite "by accident" a very beautiful woman in her early thirties, who happened to be living in Mexico City, suddenly came into my life, seemingly out of nowhere. We had a date for dinner, and she came to the apartment I stay at in Condesa when I'm in the Distrito Federal.

We never did make it to the restaurant, but wound up making love on the living room floor instead, a few feet from where I'm currently writing this book. The sex was fabulous, and it went on for six weeks. Occasionally, we would take a break to read poetry to each other, or eat an enchilada. Finally, we began to talk about moving in together; at which point, she freaked out. (She later admitted that rushing into a relationship and then rushing out was an old pattern for her.) The intimacy was too much for her, and she suffered a strong backlash: she panicked, wanted out, sent me a kind of Dear John e-mail. So the relationship ended rather abruptly, although I was left feeling more bewildered than sad. The whole incident seemed a bit too bizarre.

Some months later, at her request, we met at a café near the apartment in Condesa to exchange items we had belonging to each other: books, pictures, even shampoo (hers, not mine). She was noticeably anxious and rigid, her face set in a kind of frozen smile. She declined to sit down, refused to talk for more than two minutes, and then took off (much to her relief, I'm sure). I was a bit hurt, but I realized it was all in keeping with the behavior that had led her to say, one day, "I'll love you forever," and then the next day, to declare, "I'm outta here." Dissociation, they call it; Jekyll-and-Hyde syndrome. I realized that karmically speaking, she had a very rocky road ahead of her, the more so since there didn't appear to be a great amount of self-awareness involved.

And what did *I* get out of it? Well, six weeks of great sex with a beautiful woman, of course (nothing to sneeze at); an awareness of my own desire, still, to love and be loved; and finally, an understanding that things are just what they are: if the other person is emotionally unstable, there's very little you can do about it. (Their karma is theirs, not yours.) But there was one more thing, which I came to see shortly before that final, awkward meeting, when quite "by chance" I ran across the following poem by the American poet Mark Strand:

<u>The Coming of Light</u>

Even this late it happens:
The coming of love, the coming of light.
You wake and the candles are lit as if by themselves,
Stars gather, dreams pour into your pillows,
Sending up warm bouquets of air.
Even this late the bones of the body shine
And tomorrow's dust flares into breath.

Old bones, young spirit, I thought to myself; my dust had indeed "flared into breath." Yes, I'm alive; the world is enchanted once again.

26

Enchantment

The importance of enchantment, of magic, cannot be overestimated; and it's the one thing that is absent from all of our institutions, both public and private. I figured that out early on, which is why my relationship to institutional life has been so casual and erratic. I actually was awarded tenure at one point, and traded it in for the life of a "wandering scholar" two years later. Academic life has a very high quotient of tedium in it that can be hard to take. It also requires faculty members to devote huge amounts of time to paperwork and committee meetings that have very little to do with education. It pretty much holds true as a generalization that the one thing institutions don't wish to deal with is anything that is real (e.g., the fact that student evaluations of the professors turn the latter into entertainers, and the students wind up not learning very much). Hence, if you are someone who is interested in reality (e.g., confronting your students with questions or topics that challenge their world view and make them uncomfortable), institutional life is probably not for you.

There is a story—I don't know if it's true or not—about a meeting that was arranged between Theodor Herzl, the father of the notion of a modern Israeli homeland, and the

Pope. The Pope extended his hand for Herzl to kiss his ring; whereupon Herzl grabbed the hand, shook it, and said something along the lines of "How do you do, Pope?" I always liked that story, of how the iconoclastic Hungarian Jew gave the Pope a small dose of reality, by trying to bring His Holiness down to earth from the ethereal regions that he normally inhabited. Herzl was, of course, an exceptional person; very few individuals are going to insist on the real. More often than not it's too raw, too uncomfortable (all the more reason to pursue it).

Trusting the Center

When I say that it is important to trust, to endure, I'm talking about visceral contact, embodied contact, with your vital center. Not necessarily joy, of course; as I said, sadness is also part of the equation, which is why it is important not to run away from it or suppress it. After all, sadness is not depression—which is characterized by numbness, a lack of feeling altogether. Sadness is about loss, and loss is real for all of us at one time or another. The point is that larger forces pass through us, and it is crucial to let them do that. It may be scary, but if we don't allow this, life becomes a hollow shell. Here is a poem I wrote a couple of years ago, in a sort of trance (I can't recall what I was doing, but it just sort of spilled out), which expresses this idea. It's called "Our Bodies, Our Cars."

> I began to notice, one fine day
> that what was happening to my car
> was also happening to my body.
> A particle of dust flying into my cornea
> tears remorselessly streaming down my cheeks
> while a small stone strikes the windshield of my Chevy
> and a fracture spreads out from that point. Then
> during a prostate operation
> the pistons start malfunctioning;

the engine needs an overhaul.
Body work: don't ask...
hundreds of dollars for dents and scrapes
at the very same time that my arm becomes inflamed
and I seem to be limping around like an old man.
A tire blows on the way to the hospital
where I'm scheduled for physical therapy on my foot.
Reduced mobility, the doctor/mechanic tells me.
But then my analogy hits a wall: sure, four new tires;
but two new feet? In your dreams, says an inner voice.

My car starts to appear in my dreams, battered and tired.
"Metaphor for personality," I read in some dream book
I bought on sale in a New Age bookstore in San Francisco.
Ignition won't start: "loss of drive, purpose."
Underwater, my own Chappaquiddick: return to the
     [Unconscious.
I awake with a gasp, realizing that my therapist and my
     [mechanic
have the same last name: Aufbau, structure.
God's idea of a joke?

I sell the car, give up my mechanic and therapist,
become a man without structure
floating over the earth
like some lost-found soul in an A.R. Ammons poem—
or maybe it was Gregory Corso, I can't remember.
My dreams are filled with Vespas now, buzzing along
between small towns in Italy.
Sitting on a bench in Cortona
where Fra Angelico's angel's wings
extend beyond the boundaries of the painting
I am approached by a young boy
with a shining face
and tender eyes.
"Andiam'," he says to me.

I get up and go.

One thing I pondered, in the ensuing weeks, after I wrote this poem, was who the boy is. If the scene is taking place in a dream, then the boy is me, perhaps at a "purer" and earlier stage of my life. But if this is not a dream sequence, then it seems to me that the boy is—Christ. Not the Christ of organized religion, of course, or of American fundamentalism, both of which I regard as the death mask of Christ, the shell, which has no connection to the vital flame. No, this boy-christ is the true path of one's life, the true calling beyond any career or institution or social form. I mean, I know a "vector" when I see one; or so the poem seems to be saying.

Sunt lacrimae rerum, Virgil wrote; a very difficult phrase to translate. "Are the tears of things," literally, but a better translation might be, "The pain of the world." I am one of the privileged. I have suffered a lot, emotionally speaking, but I have never gone hungry, never been tortured or imprisoned, never been napalmed by American pilots. Some of you may be old enough to remember the famous photograph of a nine-year-old Vietnamese girl, later identified as Kim Phúc, running naked down a road in Vietnam, her body severely burned from a napalm attack. I think I first saw it on television, or in something like *Life* magazine, I'm not sure. It's an image I can't get out of my mind, and for many Americans it turned the tide of opinion regarding the war in Southeast Asia: *This* was how we were defending the United States? This butchery was protecting us from...what, exactly? The real question, of course, is how we came to such a pass that we could be dropping jellied gasoline on infants and children and actually think that it was a sensible (or even righteous) thing to do. How could it be OK to do this, even in the twisted minds of Lyndon Johnson, Robert McNamara, and Richard Nixon (who suggested the picture might be doctored—!).

37

Robopaths and Narratives

But this is what can happen when you get enslaved to a system (e.g., anti-Communism) and its accompanying slogans (e.g., "Domino Theory"): you slaughter the innocents and think it's all right. "Robopaths," the sociologist Lewis Yablonsky called such people many years ago, and the ensuing decades saw the manufacture of even more systems, slogans, and robopaths. It is this unholy trinity that causes the pain of the world, the *lacrimae rerum*, over and over and over again: Franco's torture squads, the Rape of Nanking, Hiroshima, Guantánamo. If you lose touch with yourself, with your own reality, then a huge abyss opens up in the center of your soul, and rather than sit with it, endure it, so that you can find your way home, the temptation is to stuff it with systems and slogans. Then, as a robot, you can go out and murder people by the millions, and tell yourself that you are purifying the world, making it safe for your own particular brand of truth.

Buddhism, as is well known, is designed to derail that illusion, the belief that something outside of you can make you whole. It aims to get us to look at that empty space, and the enormous desire to fill it at any price. And yet, it doesn't take much to turn Buddhism itself into a system, and Zen meditators into robots and killing machines, as Brian Victoria shows in his remarkable book, *Zen at War*, which deals with Japanese militarism prior to and during World War II. Which is to say that the road to genuine redemption may be a solitary one. Not a cheery thought, but this may be the way of the world.

It seems to me that narrative, or our need for narrative, may have a lot do with all this. In one short story by the German writer Heinrich Böll, he talks about working in an office where all of his coworkers were more interested in the story of their lives than in their lives (Facebook would be the contemporary equivalent of this). In a similar vein, Alan Watts, the great popularizer of Eastern thought, wrote about the tendency in the West to confuse the menu with the meal. I remember, when I read Böll's story many years ago—I think I was around twenty-six or twenty-seven at the time—wondering if I were not guilty of that, of wanting to precipitate events (starting an argument in a bar, smoking dope in public—that sort of thing) so I could say, "See, this is what happened to me!"

We feel naked without narrative, lost without having a story or version of our life (the more grandiose the better), and we believe that it is this—the menu rather than the actual food—that gives us sustenance, gives meaning to our daily existence. Seeing through this narrative, recognizing our need for it, understanding that it is a construct, is no easy task. After all, narrative is another word for system, which means that it is a form of pseudo-redemption—"cheating at wholeness," one might say. Of course, having a narrative is not in and of itself necessarily bad, depending on how you "carry" it. If it's a way of looking at your life ("environmental studies is something that really turns me on"), if it doesn't close you off to alternative perceptions or interpretations, all well and good. If, on the other hand, you have merged with your narrative ("I'm going to save the earth"), then you have become a robot.

Why the itch for total security? Here's another one of my poems, one which I think takes us to the core of the need for narrative:

Food Court

Nineteen years old—
a baby who made a baby.
She sits at the table,
waiting for the child
playing outside
(the Ronald McDonald thingy).
A small Barbie doll, 8" high,
lies there, abandoned, smiling
in a short skirt and high heels
looking up
at nothing in particular.
I try not to stare.
Mother, child, doll:
How fragile we all are.

The mother has an identity (narrative) as a mother; the child, in turn, clings to the Barbie doll, dresses it up and down, and fashions stories around it. This, for me, is the pain of the world, tender souls trying to cope with things as best they can, just holding it together, so to speak; and when I wrote the poem, I was on the verge of tears (lacrimae). For it is out of that fragility that we seize on "transitional objects," as they are called—dolls, blankets, teddy bears—and then eventually graduate to systems and slogans.

Confronted by alternative systems and slogans, we go to

41

pieces; we feel our very lives are at stake. So the Israeli politician doesn't want to hear about the 700,000 refugees who had to flee the country in 1948, or the children starving in Gaza today, and the Palestinian politician doesn't want to hear about the Holocaust. Psychic fragility means I can tolerate only one narrative—mine—in which I am the victim, and in which only my pain counts. This is the state of the world today.

"Progress"

In the United States the dominant narrative is "progress," by which is usually meant "freedom," by which is also meant technology or unlimited choice. (We probably manufacture forty-seven different types of razor blades by now, because we confuse novelty with creativity.) This is probably the greatest narrative ever sold; or at least, the U.S. has managed to get a lot of other countries to buy into it.

I remember reading Jonathan Franzen's novel *Freedom* about a year ago, and thinking that in many ways it was the fictionalized version of my own book *Why America Failed.* Franzen's title is an irony: the characters in it have so much freedom of choice that they are finally miserable. It's quite amazing to realize that Americans believe that having a satellite dish supplying five hundred television channels is freedom; or that the cell phone, which has turned the country into a collection of rude zombies and work-slaves, represents progress.

This narrative is more addictive than heroin, and it will not be given up until we "hit bottom," when our entire way of life comes crashing down, as I believe it eventually will. Technological innovation cannot finally give meaning to our lives, even if we did possess the resources to keep pursuing it—which we don't. A pretty good depiction of this process (or one aspect of it, anyway) occurs in another brilliant novel, *Super Sad True Love Story*, by Gary Shteyngart, which takes place about twenty years hence. By that time, precisely because of the "progress" of electronic gadgets, very few Americans bother to read anymore (or can), and certainly not "difficult" authors such as Franzen or Shteyngart. We are fast approaching the limits of our civilization, on a whole number of levels.

Roots

The fact is, we are losing our roots...we are losing everything worth anything to a homogenized, technologized culture, while actually believing it's a fabulous thing. We are especially losing our link to tradition, because today's parents are no longer in touch with it anymore, and really don't read themselves. More and more of them tend to regard books as irrelevant to their lives, and history as a meaningless subject. As a result, they have no context in which to understand what is going on around them, or to explain it to their children. They are, in short, clueless. There is an episode in the "30 Rock" comedy series in which the Alec Baldwin character goes looking for a job with some dot-com company, and his young interviewer says, "We have only one question for you: How do you propose to bring us closer to webtopia?" Tina Fey, the show's creator, is a terrific comedy writer, and her satire of the youth of America as basically morons (which she also pulled off in her film, *Mean Girls*) is as good as the famous satire she did of another outstanding moron, Sarah Palin, on Saturday Night Live. Webtopia! Now there's a narrative for you, eh?

Let me suggest a different one. I'm seven years old, and

my maternal grandfather, whose house resembles a library, regularly takes me downtown to his favorite used bookstore, where he spends three or four hours trawling through the dusty shelves, looking for "treasures." I don't mind; I love him. I sit on the floor, leafing through books that contain lots of pictures. I can read, by then, of course—I started with *Robinson Crusoe* at age three—but I'm a little kid, after all, and I like pictures of boats and castles and trains and countrysides.

A few years later, I start working my way through the *Arabian Nights*; but in the meantime, my grandfather, who speaks five languages and reads ten, decides to teach me Babylonian, which is written in cuneiform. He copies out the characters for the flood story, and explains to me that there probably was something to the story of Noah in the bible because there is a parallel version of it in the clay tablets of the Babylonians. Well, I never did manage to learn to read cuneiform, I have to admit, but I certainly did learn something about tradition and culture. As Tina Fey suggests, there is no tradition or culture in "webtopia," which is little more than a pathetic joke.

OK, I'll stop ranting; let's move on.

Desire

Although he was a bit of a charlatan, I've always been attracted to the work of the Freudian psychoanalyst Jacques Lacan because he understood the centrality of desire in human life. "Desire is the essence of man," wrote the great Jewish philosopher, Benedict Spinoza; Freud had a picture of him hanging on the wall of his study. I'm not sure Lacan really improved on Proust all that much, conceptually speaking (see below), but maybe I'm wrong. Both of them argued that desire was endless because it was always, structurally and by definition, pursing a moving target. In other words, the mechanism of desire is that of absence, of empty space (we're back to Buddhism again).

I want the desired object precisely because it eludes me, is forever out of reach, like the Grecian urn in the famous ode by John Keats. Once I attain the object of my desire, however, the attraction fades; I start looking for a new object. Somehow, it is always a *lack* of satisfaction that gets our attention, or mobilizes our energy. I've often wondered what the rate of depression is among Nobel Prize winners. I mean, where do you go from there?

"When they are interested in me, I'm not interested in them," says George Costanza, Jerry Seinfeld's kvetching side-kick, in one of the *Seinfeld* episodes. "When I'm interested in them, they are not interested in me." That's it in a nutshell, really. As Groucho Marx famously put it, "I don't want to belong to any club that will accept people like me as a member."

Form over Content

To put it another way, it's the formal properties of a situation (distance, unattainability) that constitute the deciding factor; the content is irrelevant. Literally anything can be made chic or desirable, even garbage, if people believe the object is out of their reach. There is a famous scene in Michelangelo Antonioni's film *Blow Up* in which a band leader goes crazy and smashes his guitar to pieces on the stage. The central character (played by the British actor David Hemmings) leaps onto the stage, seizes the guitar "carcass," and runs off with it, pursued by the crowd, which is convinced he is in possession of something extremely valuable. He manages to give them the slip, and standing alone in an alley, trying to catch his breath, looks at this broken piece of guitar. What is it? A useless piece of trash, really. He tosses it on the ground and walks away.

Is there any escape from this neurotic structure of desire, which all of us seem to be caught up in, and which forever prevents us from feeling whole, complete? For Proust, liberation could only come through the accidental experience of pure bodily awareness, in which the mind and body merge.

In a famous scene in *In Search of Lost Time*—arguably the greatest novel of the twentieth century—Marcel, Proust's alter ego, dips a sugary madeleine (fluted cookie) into a cup of tea, takes a bite, and suddenly, unexpectedly, the entire memory of his childhood summers in "Combray" (Illiers, in Normandy) comes flooding back into his mind, in rich detail. He writes:

> No sooner had the warm liquid, and the crumbs with it, touched my palate than a shudder ran through my whole body, and I stopped, intent upon the extraordinary changes that were taking place. An exquisite pleasure had invaded my senses, but individual, detached, with no suggestion of its origin. And at once the vicissitudes of life had become indifferent to me, its disasters innocuous, its brevity illusory—this new sensation having had on me the effect which love has of filling me with a precious essence; or rather this essence was not in me, it was myself. I had ceased now to feel mediocre, accidental, mortal.

Then, he says, "a vast structure of recollection" opened up, and

> in that moment all the flowers in our garden and in M. Swann's park, and the water-lilies on the Vivonne and the good folk of the village and their little dwellings and the parish church and the whole of Combray and all of its surroundings, taking their proper shapes and growing solid, sprang into being, town and gardens alike, from my cup of tea.

The split between mind and body collapses; the past is recaptured, as a somatic memory, and suddenly he feels whole.

The problem is that one cannot "practice" this experience, or cultivate wholeness in any organized or deliberate way. In Proust's scheme of things, the somatic breakthrough is an unexpected gift, like a mystical experience. In the case of Lacan, there was at least a technique available, namely his own idiosyncratic brand of psychoanalysis. Lacan maintained that one never got beyond transference (strong attachment to particular people, one's therapist in particular, or even certain ideas); yet for him the goal was to see through the transference, to really understand, at the deepest level (not just intellectually), that desire pursues a moving target and is therefore illusory—some version of *The Wizard of Oz*, where Dorothy learns, at the end, that she always had the power to return home, but that she needed to learn for herself that she didn't have to run away to find her heart's desire.

In his very Lacanian novel *Silk*, the Italian author Alessandro Baricco recounts the story of a Frenchman, Hervé, who pursues this will-o'-the-wisp for years, convinced that he is in love with a woman he only glimpsed on a trip he made to Japan. Nothing ever comes of it; she is really little more than a flicker of his imagination. But he devotes years of his life to that image, that faint possibility, until, when he is much older, he realizes that his whole life has been a kind of fiction. But the conclusion is not really a depressing one, as he spends his sunset years sitting by the edge of a lake, watching the waves, and reflecting on what happened—ignoring his now-dead wife for the sake of a fantasy—with a neutral kind of wisdom. The flavor of this experience, this insight, is what the Japanese call *mono no aware*—the sadness of things—which has a melancholy tone to it, and yet one of genuine acceptance as well.

If there is anything I wish I had understood about life from an early age—say, twenty at the very latest—it is this illusory quality of desire, and the tendency of the mind to favor form over content. (One wishes they would give courses in "Ontology" in high school, but I doubt that's going to happen anytime soon. It would be nice to have some insight, early on, into what makes us tick.) I suppose youth is a time for raw, unexamined experience rather than a time for reflection and insight; but to have had even a fraction of the understanding Hervé attained in later life would have been a great blessing. We are so driven, after all; and as the Buddha said, the cause of suffering is desire. Looking back, I see myself as fairly robotic, because there was virtually no distance between myself and my desires, regardless of what the desired object was. Toys, a weekend trip to the beach, ice cream—as with most kids, the list never ended, and "life" was about whatever was next on the list.

Yet it may be that a kind of "Lacanian evolution" takes place merely by getting older, even without the benefit of psychoanalysis. In other words, whereas once my focus was on the desired object, a lot of the time now it shifts to the phenomenon of desire itself. I've had the odd experience, for example, of seeing a very attractive woman in the street, or in a café, and having an aesthetic reaction rather than a sexual one: Isn't she good looking! Or if I do have a sexual response, I sometimes find myself focusing on the response itself, as an object of contemplation. This shift has been pretty new for me, a change that occurred only over the last few years. Sometimes I think it's just a case of libido slowing down with age, but I find that it takes place in nonsexual contexts as well. For example, whereas my career was, in past years, of the utmost importance to me, I find these days that I don't really have one, and I hardly ever think about it. I'm just interested in ideas, for the most part, and in sharing them with other people. Frankly, it's a relief not to be preoccupied with all that stuff anymore.

In any case, the awareness of attachment can apply to narratives as well, as I suggested earlier. Say you become capable of taking a viewpoint on your commitment to capitalism, or Communism, or Christianity, or Islam, or Existentialism, and can finally see your "ism" with some degree of detachment; after which, you are able to focus on the attachment itself. If enough of us did that, it would certainly make for a very different world. As the French diplomat Talleyrand once suggested to his countrymen, in the aftermath of The Terror (1793-94): "Above all, no zeal." Two hundred and eighteen years later, it's still good advice: we need to chill out. Or as Lincoln once put it, in the midst of the Civil War, "We must disenthrall ourselves, and then we shall save our country."

Intellectuals are particularly susceptible to this sort of narrative-blindness, going from Marxism to Existentialism to structuralism to postmodernism, all the while never realizing that what they are chasing is the next ism on the horizon—desire pursuing a moving target. What they wish to do is fix the target, and then live inside it forever. There is always the belief that they've found The Answer, until it doesn't work out, doesn't really explain what they want it to explain, and so gets replaced by The Answer II, III, IV, ad infinitum. Philosopher-longshoreman Eric Hoffer nailed this syndrome in his classic work, *The True Believer*, which is a brilliant study of this "ism addiction"; but the believers read it and assumed he was talking about *other* people and their beliefs, not themselves. This reminds me of the case of the guy stuck in traffic on the freeway and complaining about all the congestion(!). Obviously, if you are *in* the traffic, then you *are* the traffic.

62

The Authentic Life

Let's move on. Two questions come to mind at this point:

1. What does it take to live an authentic life?
2. Is it possible to have a society that supports or even encourages this?

I submit, once again, that the one thing it's possible to have in an unchanging way is awareness; and that the key to an authentic life is the awareness of your own narrative—what might be called "reflexivity." This refers to the ability to step outside your own personal belief-system and view it from the outside, as it were—as though it were someone else's belief-system, in effect.

Sociologists do this type of analysis all the time, as when they study groups of doctors, for example, or Evangelicals, or blue-collar workers, or Muncie, Indiana (Robert and Helen Lynd, *Middletown*, 1929). For the most part, however, they tend not to study sociologists, as that degree of reflexivity can be very threatening. As one wag once remarked, "There's more sociology in a department of sociology than there is in the rest of the entire world!" This would be the sociology of sociology; and if one would gather up, and study, those sociologists studying sociologists, we might call this "hyper-reflexivity," or the sociology of the sociology of sociology. (Sorry, I seem to have gone off the deep end here.)

A dramatic moment of reflexivity comes up in the film *Damage*, by Louis Malle, in which Jeremy Irons plays a character who falls so in love with a woman (played by Juliette Binoche) that he effectively turns her into his personal religion. Long after the affair is over, he accidentally sees her at an airport, from a distance—which is also a psychic distance—and he reports to the viewer: "She was no different from anyone else." This was a rare moment of sanity (reflexivity) in a life that had, even after the relationship ended, been totally organized around another person. He had endowed her with a religious quality, after all; it was hardly inherent in her, and in fact she was a rather flat, one-dimensional person, if only he had the eyes to see this. Had he stuck with this insight, that she was in fact quite ordinary, interchangeable with practically any other woman in the airport, he would have set himself on the path to an authentic life. But his attachment to the narrative of her "sacredness," her exceptionalism, was too great to resist.

Daniel Ellsberg set himself on the road to authenticity in 1971 when he realized that the Vietnam war was based on a pack of lies and so released that information to the *New York Times*, at great personal risk to himself. But a heroic example such as this can be a bit misleading. Reflexivity can also occur on a quiet and private level, and be equally authentic. Consider the teenager who was raised in a strict religious tradition—it doesn't matter which—and who slowly begins to question some of its basic tenets. This could be intellectual in nature (the questioning of religion among young people actually is intellectual, on occasion); it could also be fueled by a desire to drink, party, do drugs, and have sex (probably a lot more common). Her parents, in any case, have very little interest in this newfound reflexivity and tell her in no uncertain terms that if she continues on this path, she'll be going straight to hell.

But the questions won't go away, and eventually she understands that the religion is basically just a story, an imaginative version of how the world works. If she's aware enough, or even mature enough, she'll be able to recognize that there are good and bad aspects to the story, but that at the end of the day, it's still a narrative, with all that that implies. ("What kids are you talking about?," I can hear you saying; "it's more likely that she would construct a narrative based on becoming Kim Kardashian!" I agree, but let's not go down that depressing road just now.) She'll also be willing to "live in the question," as the German poet Rilke once put it (Keats' "negative capability"), to learn and grow rather than seize on a new narrative to replace the old one. This would be the ideal, at any rate. The Greek poet Constantine Cavafy captured the process very well in his poem, "Growing in Spirit":

> He who hopes to grow in spirit
> Will have to transcend obedience and respect.
> He will hold to some laws
> but he will mostly violate
> both law and custom, and go beyond
> the established, inadequate norm.
> Sensual pleasures will have much to teach him.
> He will not be afraid of the destructive act:
> half the house will have to come down.
> This way he will grow virtuously into wisdom.

This is as good a description of coming into authenticity as I have come across.

Heresy and Orthodoxy

Moving on to the larger issue, that of a society that encourages authenticity: that's a tough one. Historically speaking, there is a tendency for heresies to harden into orthodox-
ies. The dream of a Jewish homeland finally turns into the
nightmare of murdering Palestinian children, accompanied
by the suppression of those who object to these brutal and
destructive policies. American democracy eventually devolves
into a plutocratic charade, in which the two presidential can-
didates, Tweedledee and Tweedledum, differ only in matters
of style and are effectively bought and paid for by large cor-
porations. The larger context doesn't necessarily rule out the
search for private authenticity, but we are talking now about
the possibility of an authentic society, i.e. one that *encourages*
authenticity, and that is something that is rather hard to come
by.

In terms of societies, however, some are better and
some are worse. America used to be much more tolerant
of mavericks and creative types. For example, the twentieth
century gave us jazz and Hollywood and rock 'n' roll and Ar-
thur Miller and J.D. Salinger and etc., etc.; now, children get
drugged and sedated in elementary school, or even before
(and labeled with ever-more ingenious illnesses such Social
Anxiety Disorder, Attention Deficit Hyperactivity Disorder,

and so on, thus providing a lucrative market for the big pharmaceutical firms), while adults pop Prozac and stare into screens for much of their waking lives. As many older folks will tell you, it's not the same country that it once was.

The authentic life might be pursued in the context of certain subcultures, of course—alternate energy groups, eco-sustainable groups, "new economy" groups, or for that matter even motorcycle groups—although there is always the danger that they too might become repressive, by which I mean create another type of group narrative that everyone is required to follow. I saw a fair amount of this at a few "alternative" institutions of higher learning I taught at, where it was expected that one would use a politically correct vocabulary, utter feminist or multicultural or postmodern or ecological slogans, and "get with the program," as I was repeatedly told to do. I found it hard not to vomit. It was clear to me (if not to them) that the so-called rebel culture was as much of an ideological straightjacket as the dominant one, and in many cases, far worse. "Microfascisms," the French philosopher Gilles Deleuze called such groups, and it's hard for me to disagree. Not that subcultures *can't* produce oases of authenticity; it's just that the general tendency is to pressure members to toe the party line, which then defeats the purpose of the whole thing.

Granted, we have had a number of alternative experiments in American history that were more or less successful: Black Mountain College, for example, or the Beat Movement of the fifties and early sixties. Both produced a constellation of creative thinkers and artists, and at least for a while our society was much richer for it. Those days are over now, at least for the United States; although that doesn't prevent similar movements from arising in other places. ¡*Ojala*!, as we say Mexico.

70

Power

To talk about society at large is, at least partly, to talk about the nature of power. This issue is the central focus of one of the most important books written in recent times, namely *Your Face Tomorrow*, by the Spanish author Javier Marías. The book is a trilogy, covering more than twelve hundred pages and exploring the (a)morality of power in the modern world. The plot revolves around the adventures of Jaime Deza, the narrator and Marías' alter ego, who goes to work for an "invisible" British agency that may or may not be attached to MI5 or MI6, the British intelligence services. Jaime is hired to sit in on, or observe, interviews of various people and "read" their personalities for his employer. He has no idea what the information will be used for, although given the nature of the interviews it is pretty clear that high stakes are involved, both military and diplomatic.

Jaime's boss, Bertram Tupra, is purely amoral: his philosophy boils down to "might makes right," or "whatever it takes to accomplish your goals"; and in one memorable scene he beats a man senseless in the bathroom of a discotheque because the guy was creating an embarrassing situation for an important client of the organization. Jaime himself, towards the end of the trilogy, is led to imitate this behavior, scaring off his wife's lover by brutalizing him—crippling his left hand by beating it with an iron poker. This changes his narrative of himself, because up to then he believed that he would never compromise his principles for the sake of personal advantage. But prior to this, he has it out with Tupra, in the wake of the bathroom incident, telling him, "You can't just go around beating people up." "Why not?," asks Tupra, quite seriously; and Jaime finally replies (later on in the story), "Because then it would be impossible for anyone to live." Which is true, but in the context of the discussion it has no weight, and comes off as rather lame. I'll return to this in a moment, but first let me give you a little background material.

It turns out that Javier's father, Julián Marías, was a prominent Spanish philosopher from the 1930s on (he died in 2005). Since he had Republican sympathies, he ran afoul of the Franco regime in the wake of the Spanish Civil War. He was imprisoned at one point, and banned from teaching in Spain for more than two decades. Nevertheless, he was lucky, given the usual practice of torture and assassination meted out to political liberals by Franco's goons, who certainly had no qualms about going around beating people up. Through his father's experience, Javier learned the meaning of *Realpolitik*; Tupra's philosophy, that life was about power and not much else, was hardly new to him.

Yet it is not that simple, because Julián Marías was a disciple of the great Spanish philosopher Ortega y Gasset, who in turn had gone to Germany in the early years of the twentieth century to study philosophy, and who became a major proponent of Neo-Kantian thought. When Jaime tells Tupra that one can't go around beating people up because "it would be impossible for anyone to live," this is in fact what Kant referred to as the "categorical imperative." As a moral

74

rule, Kant posited the notion that no action should be undertaken if it could not be generalized to society at large.

This, then, is the source of the tension in *Your Face Tomorrow*, because the categorical imperative is purely exhortatory: it has no *power* to compel people to behave morally, and this is why Jaime's response, at first glance, seems weak. Tupra, after all, is talking about the world as it actually is, not as it should be. Jaime wants, à la Kant, to have a moral rule that would apply to large-scale social behavior, and this can only fall flat in the face of *Realpolitik*–precisely the thing that had destroyed Julián Marías' career, and almost his life. An individual answer would be much more convincing: "It's a question of what kind of life you want to lead, isn't it? It's a question of what you want the narrative of your life to be." To which Tupra might have just grunted, or perhaps shrugged, since he had made up his mind on that issue a long time ago.

Dopamine

I recently decided to reread *Your Face Tomorrow*, and as I got to the end of the first volume I took a break, went to sleep, and had a horrible nightmare. In the dream I was some sort of nurse or medical assistant, working with a patient, and was suddenly criticized publicly by another medical assistant for not knowing something about drugs—dopamine in particular (it's actually a chemical in the brain, a neurotransmitter). It was humiliating, and I became so enraged that I began punching my critic in the face until the entire front of my lab coat was covered with his blood.

At this point, things become a little blurry, but here is what I think happened: I awoke momentarily from the dream in a state of horror, that I could do this, and then I returned to the dream and apologized profusely to the man I had beaten up, very much ashamed of what I had done. Or else, I apologized first, without waking up from the dream, and then woke up after the apology—but still in a state of revulsion over my actions.

Either way, the horror, the revulsion, came partly out of the fact that even if I could just dream this, even if I had never done something like this in waking life, it nevertheless violated the narrative I have of myself as an essentially well-meaning and nonviolent person; what Jaime believed about himself until he crippled his wife's lover with an iron poker. After all, there is no getting around the fact that this potential violence is in my unconscious, buried in a primitive part of my psyche, one that couldn't care less about Kant and the categorical imperative any more than Tupra did. It was a dream I would have preferred not to have had, because it disrupted the narrative of myself as someone incapable of such behavior.

Why dopamine? The other medic called me out for not knowing the effects of dopamine, which I mistakenly related to aspirin, in the dream. The next morning, when I was fully awake, I went online and looked it up in Wikipedia. Did I somehow know this prior to having the dream, or before re-reading Volume 1 of *Your Face Tomorrow*? It seems too perfect. Dopamine is a neurotransmitter within the part of the brain responsible for reward-driven learning. According to the "dopaminergic mind hypothesis," I read, the "high-dopamine personality" is characterized by "high intelligence, a sense of personal destiny [strong narrative], a religious/cosmic preoccupation [also strong narrative], an obsession with achieving goals and conquests, [and] an emotional detachment that in many cases leads to ruthlessness." It is thus possible that high levels of it underlie the increased psychological disorders of modern society. A "dopaminergic society" is an "extremely goal-oriented, fast-paced, and even manic society"— sociopathic, in other words. Individuals with high dopamine levels lack empathy, and societies with high levels of it are characterized by competition and aggression, rather than by nurturance and community—a good description of America, wouldn't you say?

The footnotes to this article led me to the work of one Fred Previc, author of *The Dopaminergic Mind in Human Evo-*

lution and History. Previc studied the role of dopamine in human evolution, and concluded that the "dopaminergic mind" may no longer be adaptive to the health of the human race or the planet in general—Kant's categorical imperative—and that high dopamine levels can lead to social dysfunction, including "endless wars and conquests" and detachment and alienation from other human beings. The dopaminergic society, claims Previc, is the dopaminergic personality writ large, primarily characterized by a lack of empathy. We are, he concludes, living in a situation of "dopamine gone wild." (A *Newsweek* cover story in July 2012 suggested that the Web was driving Americans crazy, and increasing the dopamine levels in their brains. So much for "webtopia.")

Of course, I'm skeptical as to whether individual human behavior, let alone large-scale social behavior, can be explained in such a reductionistic way; it seems far too facile. Still, I feel that Previc may be onto something, providing a kind of biochemical variation on Kant. You really *can't* go around beating people up whenever it suits your purposes because the logical endpoint is the destruction of the human race: as Jaime says, it would be impossible to live. Tupra's rhetorical "Why not?" makes sense only in the short term, i.e. within the logic of immediate advantage. This is certainly how MI5, MI6, the CIA, and the Mafia operate; but on a large scale we are now experiencing "blowback" as a result—terrorism, environmental degradation, the loss of meaning in industrial (or virtual-cybernetic) societies, the replacement of love between men and women by fear...dopamine gone wild, in short.

This way of life, this narrative that we have been living with for several hundred years now (the "arc" of capitalism, as it's called in World Systems Analysis), is fast coming to a close, and we shall be forced to adopt a different sort of narrative whether we like it or not. After all, the categorical imperit-would seem to to be a variation on the Golden Rule, and we probably cannot violate it indefinitely.

Spinning Straw into Gold

Well, Gentle Reader, we've wandered into rather murky territory, have we not? It's not clear what else remains to be said at this point. We've talked about "vectors," and finding one's own way in the world, and about magic, authenticity, and the importance of trust. We also talked about narratives, how best to handle them, and the importance of not turning them into objects of worship. And we've spent some time on love, desire, and power. That would seem to exhaust the world, more or less. As for society, I doubt there's much more we can say about it; America, at least, is collapsing from its own dopamine addiction (if that is what is actually operative; it certainly works as a metaphor, in any case), and several other nations are likely to follow suit. Maybe we should return briefly to the issue of individual spirituality, before going our separate ways.

Remember the little dwarf in *Grimm's Fairy Tales*, Rumpelstiltskin, who was able to spin straw into gold? That's what I believe we are here on this earth to do. Again, it all comes down to what you want your life to be about. It can't be about power *and* about healing your soul, your society, your culture, or the world (*tikkun olam*, in Hebrew); the two are mutually exclusive. Nurturance and competition are not merely two different types of behavior; they are also two different mindsets, two contradictory ways of being in the world. The latter will ultimately rot your soul, destroy your life from within.

> Ach, wie gut, dass niemand weiss,
> dass ich Rumpelstilzchen heiss!
>
> How good it is that no one knows,
> that I am called Rumpelstiltskin!

This was the secret word, the one that made it possible for the miller's daughter to spin the straw into gold (that is, to get Rumpelstiltskin to do it for her, and not have to surrender her first-born child to him later on). Exactly what the gold is for each of us individually is not important; all that matters is that we all have it within us.

There are so many forces trying to get you to live in a narrative not of your own making, to betray yourself, to forfeit everything really important to you so that you can fit in. Isn't it exhausting, working long hours at a meaningless job, sucking up to a boss you hate, taking antidepressants to get through the day, and telling everyone at work that you are happy to be there? Doesn't it nag at you, that you have a large house filled with expensive objects while you never have sex with your spouse anymore, and your kids don't talk to you and just sit in their rooms playing video games? Isn't it disturbing to you that you have no real friends, but just people in your environment with whom you share nothing deep and personal, whom you don't trust, and with whom you have virtually nothing in common?

And beyond that, what does it feel like to live in a culture in which power and influence mean nothing more than this: that one is willing to inject poison into its veins on a daily basis? This is what gets rewarded in our society (just look around!); and in a psychosocial version of what is known in economics as Gresham's Law (bad currency drives good currency out of circulation), it's the garbage that floats to the top. Is this what you want your life to be about? After all, it's going to be over faster than you can blink, and you are going to be dead for a very long time.

You

What is *your* secret word, then? What is that glimpse or vector or bit of understanding that can get you to start spinning straw into gold? Do you know what it is? If not, how do you propose to find out, assuming you want to step out of your narrative and start living an authentic life? Of course, *I* don't have that word for you; I have enough trouble searching for my own. The fact is that no guru, no system, no slogan, no narrative, no Barbie doll, no transitional object, has it for you; you will have to look elsewhere to find it, perhaps in some unusual and uncomfortable places ("half the house will have to come down").

And you probably won't find it right away, either. But hey, there's no rush, and living in limbo won't kill you (even if you think it will). The end of your world, to paraphrase Mark Strand, is not the end of the world as such, but only the end of the world as you know it. And that could be a good thing, after all; maybe, even, the best thing imaginable.

So good luck, my friend; perhaps I'll see you on the farther shore.

Mexico City
13-14 July 2012

ABOUT THE AUTHOR

Morris Berman is a poet, novelist, essayist, social critic, and cultural historian. He has written fourteen books and more than one hundred and fifty articles, and has taught at a number of universities in Europe, North America, and Mexico. He won the Governor's Writers Award for Washington State in 1990, and was the first recipient of the annual Rollo May Center Grant for Humanistic Studies in 1992. In 2000, *The Twilight of American Culture* was named a "Notable Book" by the *New York Times Book Review*, and in 2013 he received the Neil Postman Award for Career Achievement in Public Intellectual Activity from the Media Ecology Association. Dr. Berman lives in Mexico.

BY THE SAME AUTHOR

Social Change and Scientific Organization

Trilogy on human consciousness:
The Reenchantment of the World
Coming to Our Senses
Wandering God: A Study in Nomadic Spirituality

Trilogy on the American empire:
The Twilight of American Culture
Dark Ages America: The Final Phase of Empire
Why America Failed: The Roots of Imperial Decline

A Question of Values (essays)
Destiny (fiction)
Counting Blessings (poetry)

Neurotic Beauty: An Outsider Looks at Japan
The Man Without Qualities (fiction)

Colophon

Text and Titles: Goudy Old Style
Set in Adobe Indesign

CPSIA information can be obtained
at www.ICGtesting.com
Printed in the USA
BVOW05s1344040617
485622BV00020B/93/P